The GRAND MEMORY WAVE series began with a precious personal family experience. My dad had just passed from life here on earth into God's hands. The funeral home directors put Dad's body into the hearse and began driving down our long farm driveway. Just as the hearse was ready to take off, my heart jumped into my throat. I knew that we needed to give Dad a "GRAND WAVE".

   You need to know that over all the years of my life our family has been notorious for our grand waves. The "grand wave" consists of all the family members together jumping up and down, waving hands, and yelling our loving goodbyes as the family members leaving drive off. As we wave, we are remembering the times we've had together.

   Tearfully I waved and jumped. At the same time, my heart also soared! Dad was dead, but God made this moment VICTORIOUS. It was true. Death was swallowed up in eternal life. I knew God was with Dad and with all of us.

   I felt called by God to ask other people to share their experiences of a time when they knew that God was with them. The responses in this book are a collection of personal experiences from people of all ages witnessing to God's presence.

   The goal was to have each person's response 10 words or less. When I first began to collect them, I questioned God about gathering such short responses from people. I felt as though such an offering would be too little for such an awesome God who promises to be with us always.

   In Job 38 verses 6 and 7, God paints a picture that I cannot get out of my mind. While God is laying the foundation of the world, we are told, *"All the morning stars sang together and all the angels shouted for joy"*. God was assuring me through this passage that even short responses would sing God's praises.

I knew that the subtitle for volume one of the GRAND MEMORY WAVE book and series needed to be, *While the Morning Stars Sang Together and All the Angels Shouted for Joy.* It is my aim to keep collecting and publishing recollections of God's presence in the lives of God's people. May the sharing of God's presence in our lives be a great GRAND MEMORY WAVE back to God!

****

This book is dedicated to Dad and to my extended family, the original "grand wave" crew.

Thanks go to the members of Mt. Olive Lutheran Church who were the first to respond.

Special thanks go to Kitty Pityer and to my family, Paul, Sarah, Rachel and Nathan, for their editorial skills.
****

I know/knew that God is/was with me when…

I heard Muslim, Jewish and Christian voices joined in praise.
Megham

I watched teenagers find the sacred in a beautiful sunrise.
Amy

I heard my husband and son's laughter as they played.
Katherine

Jesus gave His Body and Blood to forgive my sins.
David

I was extremely sick and coughing, but did not die.
Amber, Lenoir-Rhyne, North Carolina

He healed me of depression and made me smile again.
Kelli

I first gazed into my newborn daughter's eyes.
Andrea

I finally revealed to the world how broken I was.
Grace

I finally shared my fears about my father's health problems.
Ashley

I finally lost weight and felt better about myself.
Brandon

A blind youth courageously climbed a tower just by feel.
Carrie

Jesus dying for my sins was fully explained to me.
Wade

My pastor shared my grief at my great-grandmother's graveside.
Tammy

My six-year-old son asked me, "Dad, if Jesus is God, then who is He talking to when He is praying?"
Chad

I'm driving by myself in the dark.
Erica, Age 17, Raleigh, North Carolina

All the time!
Nicole, Age 13, Cary, North Carolina

I made the tennis team.
Thomas, Age 15

I got into fights with my friends.
Chelsea, Age 15, Lewisville, North Carolina

My daughter was born.
Mark, Age 49, Cary, North Carolina

I battled cancer.
Carol, Age 45, Greensboro, North Carolina

My grandfather died!
Jessie, Age 14, Greensboro, North Carolina

I was scared.
Karoline, Age 13, Greensboro, North Carolina

My grandpa died.
Janie, Age 15, Greensboro, North Carolina

I needed His help.
Caroline, Age 13, Greensboro, North Carolina

I look at His creation.
Katie-Bess, Age 14, Greensboro, North Carolina

My hamster died.
Michele, Age 16, Albemarle, North Carolina

My pet died on the first day of school.
Elizabeth, Age 12, Cary, North Carolina

I was having a hard time getting over Grandma's death.
Marcella, Age 11, Raleigh, North Carolina

I was born.
Nick, Age 11, Greensboro, North Carolina

I broke my arm.
Michael, Age 14, Greensboro, North Carolina

The finest Christian parents any man could have adopted me.
Scott, Age 43, Greensboro, North Carolina

I saw a smile on everyone's face.
Bryan, Age 16, Greensboro, North Carolina

Dad died.
Leonard, Salisbury, North Carolina

I need Him.
Austin, Age 20, Albemarle, North Carolina

I'm faced with a difficult time or decision.
Courtney, Age 17, Raleigh, North Carolina

He helped me through my broken arm.
Hunter, Age 14, Raleigh, North Carolina

I try to make decisions.
Marissa, Age 17, Cary, North Carolina

I was in the hospital.
Caroline, Age 17, Cary, North Carolina

I started in youth ministry 25 years ago and had no idea what I was doing.
Nesta, Age "young at heart," Vale, North Carolina

All through my life.
Allison, Age 14, Climax, North Carolina

I was close to death after my appendix ruptured.
Myrtle, Age 40, Greensboro, North Carolina

My mom had breast cancer.
Alice, Age 46, Raleigh, North Carolina

I went to Cruzando in San Antonio, Texas.
Julie, Age 16, Winston-Salem, North Carolina

Whenever I make a move in my life.
Beth Ann, Age 17, Charlotte, North Carolina

A drunk driver almost hit me.
Garrett, Age 16, Salisbury, North Carolina

My dad had a heart attack when I was six.
Lindsey, Age 17, Kannapolis, North Carolina

My good friend died.
Karleah, Age 17, Kannapolis, North Carolina

My wife and I decided to move to North Carolina.
Andy, Age 37, Raleigh, North Carolina

A machine was breathing for my 15-day-old son.
Mandy, Age 35, Raleigh, North Carolina

He made me realize all I had even after I had lost so much.
Olivia, Age 16, Vale, North Carolina

He helped my family through surgery.
Hampton, Age 11, Raleigh, North Carolina

I fell hard on the concrete and got right up.
Philip, Age 16, Raleigh, North Carolina

All the time.
Mitchell, Age 11, Raleigh, North Carolina

I play sports.
Josh, Age 16, Hickory, North Carolina

My grandmother Zela died.
Age 15, Hickory, North Carolina

I was born.
Leslie, Age 15, Raleigh, North Carolina

I looked on God's creation at Niagara Falls.
Elizabeth, Age 14, Indian Trail, North Carolina

I stared into the eyes of my new niece.
Rachel, Age 16, Hickory, North Carolina

My dad was about to die.
Samantha, Age 15, Matthews, North Carolina

I had to tell my children their grandfather had passed away.
Eric, Age 52, Hickory, North Carolina

My grandparents passed away.
Meredith, Age 17, Matthews, North Carolina

My grandpa was in the hospital.
Paul, Age 15, Matthews, North Carolina

I thought about ending my life.
Courtney, Age 16, Mills River, North Carolina

My brother died.
Brent, Age 16, Matthews, North Carolina

My aunt passed away due to cancer.
Emily, Age 13, Matthews, North Carolina

I passed the computer test.
Adam, Age 14, Matthews, North Carolina

I went to Park Ridge Elementary for the first time.
Aaron, Age 12, Charlotte, North Carolina

I gave birth to triplets eight weeks early.
Lisa, Age 47, Salisbury, North Carolina

I was in San Antonio.
Dylan, Age 17, Faith, North Carolina

My dad quit using drugs.
Ryan, Age 15, Kannapolis, North Carolina

My son passed away.
Sara, Age 32, Kannapolis, North Carolina

I was applying for college.
Katie, Age 17, Kannapolis, North Carolina

I'm in the woods.
Erick, Age 17, Apex, North Carolina

I was left alone and frightened, I prayed for God's care.
Florence, Age 53, Concord, North Carolina

At LYO.
Madeline, Age 12, Kannapolis, North Carolina

I had cancer when I was younger.
Caleb, Age 13, Kannapolis, North Carolina

I prayed for my dog to be released from pain. He died a few minutes later, but God granted me peace.
Kelly, Age 16, Lumberton, North Carolina

My husband was told he might have brain tumors. We prayed. They found only an safely sealed "encapsulated" tumor.
Anne, Age 44, Lumberton, North Carolina

My grandma felt really sick and my prayers helped her. God helped me learn that He is always there.
Melissa, Age 12, Lumberton, North Carolina

I flew after 9-11.
Sara, Age 13, Hickory, North Carolina

I went to camp for the first time.
Mandy, Age 12, Bethlehem, North Carolina

We had a lockdown at my school.
Matthew, Age 13, Hickory, North Carolina

I was nearly in a bad car accident.
Blake, Age 18, Charlotte, North Carolina

My son was born.
Shane, Age 31, Annapolis, North Carolina

I'm going through a difficult time in my life.
Holly, Age 17, Cary, North Carolina

I struggle to talk around people I'm uncomfortable with.
Kevin, Age 17, Apex, North Carolina

I met people at my youth group.
Gabriele, Age 17, Cary, North Carolina

I make tough decisions.
Colleen, Age 17, Raleigh, North Carolina

I confessed at STWTEC in a circle prayer.
Nathaniel, Age 17, Cary, North Carolina

I got involved in OTK and TEC.
Grace, Age 15, Cary, North Carolina

I felt called to participate in my church's servant camp.
Annette, Age 14, Cary, North Carolina

I'm at school.
Anna, Age 13, Annapolis, North Carolina

My aunt got really sick and almost died.
Sarah, Age 13, Annapolis, North Carolina

The sun rises.
Kara, Age 17, Holly Springs, North Carolina

I prayed for my mother's strength.
Chris, Age 15, Salisbury, North Carolina

I was diagnosed with diabetes at age 10.
Kayla, Age 17, Faith, North Carolina

I was born.
Hannah, Age 16, Salisbury, North Carolina

My friend was going through hard times and with God's help, I helped her through it.
Marisa, Age 16, Faith, North Carolina

Whenever I wrestle.
Every time I wrestle.
Kyle, Age 16, Charlotte, North Carolina

My mom had surgery.
Jesse, Age 16, Charlotte, North Carolina

I had my first dance competition.
Megan, Age 12, Hickory, North Carolina

My parents divorced.
Courtney, Age 17, Southern Pines, North Carolina

I seek Him.
Ty, Age 17, Fuquay-Varina, North Carolina

I'm in trouble.
Nick, Age 12, Holly Springs, North Carolina

I get a hug. It feels like the arms of God are wrapped around me.
Charlie, Age 28, Fuquay, North Carolina

I got a position on the LYO Eastern Cluster Board.
Cassie, Age 15, Holly Springs, North Carolina

I read the Bible.
David, Age 16, Concord, North Carolina

I was trying out for the school's swim team.
Carly, Age 14, Holly Springs, North Carolina

My children were born.
Carol, Age 55, Clemmons, North Carolina

I began my Confirmation journey.
Russell, Age 15, Greensboro, North Carolina

I was born with fluid in my lungs.
Jeri, Age 12, Hendersonville, North Carolina

My sons were born.
Adam, Age 34, Indian Trail, North Carolina

I am into my youth!
Liz, Youth Director, Age 31, Matthews, North Carolina

My grandfather had a heart attack.
Matthew, Age 13, Charlotte, North Carolina

We had a tornado.
Eric, Age 12, Vale, North Carolina

I experienced a friend's death and my Grandpa's diagnosis.
Adam, Age 14, Vale, North Carolina

I was going through the deaths of my granddad and my friend.
Dylan, Age 14, Vale, North Carolina

I broke my arm.
Corey, Age 16, Matthews, North Carolina

I cried out to Him and He answered me with a rainbow in my path.
Teresa, Age 38, Matthews, North Carolina

My mom died.
Donna, Age 42, Charlotte, North Carolina

I was choking on ice.
Taylor, Age 13, Matthews, North Carolina

I was coming here.
Matt, Age 13, Fuquay-Varina, North Carolina

I was taken to the hospital.
Samantha, Age 16, Fuquay-Varina, North Carolina

I got in trouble for stuff in school I didn't do and needed Him to get me through it.
Matt, Age 15, Holly Springs, North Carolina

I was at LYO.
Mandy, Age 17, Matthews, North Carolina

I pray.
Adam, Age 17, Charlotte, North Carolina

He helped me when my friend moved.
Katelyn, Age 16, Etowah, North Carolina

I was given a little brother.
Garrett, Age 15, Matthews, North Carolina

I moved to North Carolina.
Lucas, Age 14, Indian Trail, North Carolina

I'm praying.
Cosmo, Age 12, Matthews, North Carolina

We all sing in a big group.
Elisa, Age 18, Southern Pines, North Carolina

When I was baptized in the water.
Ben, Age 17, Southern Pines, North Carolina

My grandfather died.
Ethan, Age 18, Vale, North Carolina

My friend died in a car accident.
Diana, Age 18, West End, North Carolina

I flew my first mission to Baghdad.
Ryan, Age 32, Southern Pines, North Carolina

My great aunt died.
Garrett, Age 17, Vale, North Carolina

I had my car wreck.
Marty, Age 18, Albemarle, North Carolina

I was baptized
Aola, Age 12, Hendersonville, North Carolina

I do crazy things with my friends.
Morgan, Age 12, Indian Trail, North Carolina

I am sad and angry.
Becca, Age 12, Henderson, North Carolina

I went to workcamp in Mississippi and learned to dry wall.
Kelli Jo, Age 15, Hendersonville, North Carolina

I was at TEC.
Leigh, Age 15, Hendersonville, North Carolina

I was scared.
Josh, Age 9, Winston-Salem, North Carolina

I watched my friend get baptized at age 16.
Joy, Age 15, Mills River, North Carolina

My days shined more.
Cordi, Age 11, Albemarle, North Carolina

Our daughter was born.
Anne, Age 48, Albemarle, North Carolina

My children were born.
Mark, Age 36, Winston-Salem, North Carolina

I least expect it.
Sarah, Age 19, Tobaccoville, North Carolina

He shows up and shows out. He continues to answer my prayers in many, many ways.
Linda, Age 58, Durham, North Carolina

Always.
Andrew, Age 15, Raleigh, North Carolina

I arrived here safely.
Nic, Age 18, Kannapolis, North Carolina

My Kyle memorial bracelet was returned when it was lost.
Alli, Age 14

My grandfather passed away.
Thomas, Age 17, Lenoir, North Carolina

I ask to be filled with the Holy Spirit to serve Him according to His will.
Steve, Age 51, Lenoir, North Carolina

I deployed to Iraq.
Paul, Age 40, Harrisburg, North Carolina

I rode my bike without training wheels.
Colleen, Age 17, Charlotte, North Carolina

I moved my family to North Carolina.
Mark, Age 50, Charlotte, North Carolina

I went to San Antonio, Texas, and it was my first time flying.
Brittany, Age 18, Charlotte, North Carolina

I first tried carrot cake!
Katie, Age 16, Concord, North Carolina

My grandfather (Paw) died.
Brandon, Age 13, Lenoir, North Carolina

He kept me safe and protected me through a horrible car accident.
Erin, Age 24, Concord, North Carolina

I asked for His help.
Christine, Age 15, Charlotte, North Carolina

When I came here.
Brad, Age 13, Charlotte, North Carolina

I am at LYOs.
Chelsea, Age 14, Charlotte, North Carolina

All the time.
Lesley, Age 26, Charlotte, North Carolina

He died for me on the cross.
Hilary, Age 16, Charlotte, North Carolina

My dad had to get surgery.
Harrison, Age 14, Charlotte, North Carolina

I prayed for something and it came true!
Rachel, Age 14, Charlotte, North Carolina

I prayed when my best friend's dad almost passed away.
Meredith, Age 15, Concord, North Carolina

My friend found me in the darkness.
Jared, Age 17, Clemmons, North Carolina

When I drive. He was there when I almost wrecked.
Zack, Age 15, Clemmons, North Carolina

My grandmother died.
Courtney, Age 11, Matthews, North Carolina

My grandparents passed away.
Ethan, Age 17, Faith, North Carolina

I comforted a friend through a hard time.
Emily, Age 18, Winston-Salem, North Carolina

A peer older than me died in a car wreck.
Elizabeth, Age 17, Lenoir, North Carolina

I came to LYO!
Dillon, Age 17, Albermarle, North Carolina

My dad died.
Rachel, Age 17, Wake Forest, North Carolina

I ask for help making decisions.
Marissa, Age 16, Raleigh, North Carolina

I moved to North Carolina from Pennsylvania for my first call as pastor.
June, Age 33, Lumberton, North Carolina

He healed my liver when I was newly born.
Matthew, Age 17, Greensboro, North Carolina

I broke my neck for the third time.
Jake, Age 17, Shelby, North Carolina

I was six.
Tre, Age 13, Sanford, North Carolina

I was saved from drowning by a friend in high school.
Tom, Age 44, Sanford, North Carolina

I had my children.
Holly, Age 44, Sanford, North Carolina

I was three.
John, Age 11, Sanford, North Carolina

At all times, when things are going well and when there are trying times.
Levi, Age 60, Hickory, North Carolina

I transported and cared for critical neonatal and pediatric patients and their families.
Eva, Age 57, Taylorsville, North Carolina

God was with me when I got married, and brought my two babies into this world.
Monica, Age 26, Taylorsville, North Carolina

Each of our three children was born.
Odell, Age 82, Hickory, North Carolina

My husband was dying and I felt His guidance.
Pat, no age, Hickory, North Carolina

I see the cross.
Dave, North Carolina

I see the morning sun and other works of creation.
Mark, North Carolina

I walk, pray and read on the treadmill.
Karen, Age 53, Hickory, North Carolina

My church family shares my pain over my daughter's illness.
The Christian community at Mt. Olive shares my pain in the illness of my daughter.
Hickory, North Carolina

My mother rose to life eternal and was healed.
Jean, Hickory, North Carolina

My children were born and later at their baptism.
Nancy, Age 76, Hickory, North Carolina

Each day I am allowed to enjoy the world and people He created.
Glenn, Age 77, Hickory, North Carolina

I experienced the wonder of giving birth to my child. What a miracle! *Mary Beth, Hickory, North Carolina*

I see the joy in children's faces as their parents pick them up from day care and school.
Naomi, Age 59, no city

My mother passed.
Lillian, Age 79, Hickory, North Carolina

I listen in prayer and that "still, small voice" responds.
Ruth, Age 77, Hickory, North Carolina

I go to church.
Rachel, Age 10, Hickory, North Carolina

I visit my mother who was diagnosed with Alzheimer's.
Nina, Age 46, Hickory, North Carolina

Each and every time I receive a letter from one of the "compassion" children my husband and I sponsor.
Susan

I see car headlights turning into our driveway.
Libby, Age 53, Hickory, North Carolina

My two daughters and grandson were born.
Bob, Age 55, Hickory, North Carolina

God sent an angel to rescue me from a Wisconsin snowstorm.
Judean, Age 63, Bangor, Wisconsin

He gave my dying husband time to spend with family.
Annie, Age 65, Rockland, Wisconsin

He spoke a message to me from my dying father.
Donna, Age 50, Milwaukee, Wisconsin

I was raising my children to know God.
Nancy, Age 68, Westby, Wisconsin

I found peace through prayer before a heart transplant.
Anna Marie, Age 68, Gays Mills, Wisconsin

My mother passed away at the very end of my father's funeral.
Marilyn, Age 71, Viroqua, Wisconsin

Dad died and I graduated from college and taught children.
Lois, Age 71, Sparta, Wisconsin

A former student sat with me during my husband's surgery.
Janice, Age 75, Coon Valley, Wisconsin

My children were born and everyone turned out very well.

My husband was shouting. God said I'd be all right.
Beverly, Age 78, Westby, Wisconsin

I saw a bright light that was Jesus.
June, Age 80, Prairie du Chien, Wisconsin

My husband was killed in an accident.

I became a grandmother after a very long wait.
Carlene, Age 65, Camp Douglas, Wisconsin

I faced breast cancer without fear.
My father was killed in a tractor accident in 1964.
Lorraine, Age 79, La Crosse, Wisconsin

I walked away from a serious car accident unharmed.

My son moved to Korea to work and live.
Cheryl, Age 62, Holmen, Wisconsin

When I had my heart surgery.
Meliea, Viroqua, Wisconsin

He gave me strength to get through my husband's death.
Mira, Age 76, Onalaska, Wisconsin

My healthy Mom was suddenly taken from our family in a 2004 car accident.

A nurse baptized our newborn son before he died.
Norma, Age 63, Blair, Wisconsin

He answered my prayer of fear with a song.
Julie, Age 34, Tomah, Wisconsin

I sat with my family to accept the word "cancer."
Sonya, Age 65, De Soto, Wisconsin

I missed an accident with an oil truck by seconds.
Lorraine, Age 70, Chaseburg, Wisconsin

In a vision, God said, "I am with you always."
Yvonne, Age 74, La Crosse, Wisconsin

I walked with our sisters and brothers in Ethiopia.
JoAnn, Age 66, New Lisbon, Wisconsin

His strength helped us survive our son's accidental death.
Myra, Age 77, Chaseburg, Wisconsin

I witnessed the miraculous birth of our first grandchild.
Joan, Age 62, La Crescent, Minnesota

I had five heart bypasses.
Marilyn, Age 72, Ettrick, Wisconsin

I get up each morning. He walks with me daily.
Cleo, Age 81, Viroqua, Wisconsin

My mother saw visions of heaven before she passed away.
Mary Ann, Age 79, Galesville, Wisconsin

He guided our family from Illinois to our Wisconsin dairy farm in 1977.
JoAnn, Age 70, Viroqua, Wisconsin

I enjoy his beautiful creation.
Karen, Age 65, Viroqua, Wisconsin

I attended my first National Convention at Detroit, Michigan.
Beverly, Age 76, Viroqua, Wisconsin

I faced breast cancer without fear.
Sara, Age 76, Kendall, Wisconsin

Surgery complications were corrected through the intervention of the nurse.
Effie, Age 64, La Crosse, Wisconsin

I was singing at Luther Park Bible Camp.
Pauline, Age 59, Sparta, Wisconsin

We found a house in the country with beautiful trees.
Annette, Age 69, Tomah, Wisconsin

My husband was seriously injured in a private plane crash.
Arlene, Westby, Wisconsin

I had breast cancer surgery.

I observed the birth of my great-granddaughter.
Mona, Age 66, Spring Grove, Minnesota

He sent me His peace vis-à-vis my chosen profession.
Mary, Age 63, Viroqua, Wisconsin

I'm working outside and see His peace and beauty.

--God assured me He'd make the right decision regarding my granddaughter's life.
Vivian, Age 79, Ettrick, Wisconsin

I was recovering from serious heart surgery.

I was 17, pregnant and alone in a big city.

My grandmother shared her faith with me as she died.
Kristin, Age 30, Ettrick, Wisconsin

A rainbow assured me of God's presence during my father's surgery. *Mary Jo, Age 67, Arcadia, Wisconsin*

I experienced the deaths of my husband and daughter. *Gertie, Age 81, Ettrick, Wisconsin*

My great-grandson was baptized.

I have felt God's presence in my life since I was about 13. *Connie, Age 69, West Salem, Wisconsin*

I had brain surgery in 1992. *LaVerne, Age 82, La Crosse, Wisconsin*

My father went into cardiac arrest but was saved. *Shari, Age 46, Mindoro, Wisconsin*

We had to give our first grandson back to God. *Carol, Age 63, Mauston, Wisconsin*

I was diagnosed with lymphoma Stage IV after breast cancer. *Linda, Age 60, La Crosse, Wisconsin*

My oldest daughter was killed by a drunk driver. *Norma, Age 90, Sparta, Wisconsin*

In one year, my parents died, my son was born and my marriage failed; yet God was there. *Ann, Age 58, Viroqua*

I witnessed the birth of my first grandchild. *Elaine, Age 63, Bessemer City, North Carolina*

I survived the fire bombing of Dresden, Germany in 1945. *Harald, Age 68, Aberdeen, North Carolina*

I was 8 and found a church in my neighborhood.
Margie, Age 62, Charlotte, North Carolina

My husband died and I had peace that passes understanding.
Janet, Age 54, Vale, North Carolina

I was on my first trip to Belarus.
Janet, Age 54, Vale, North Carolina

The doctor told me that I would not need chemotherapy.
Suzanne, Age 62, Raleigh, North Carolina

I felt peace as my husband passed into His presence.
Valerie, Age 75, Raleigh, North Carolina

I look at my young child asleep with arms outstretched.
Hobby, Age 41, Kings Mountain, North Carolina

My pastor challenged me to consider going to seminary.
George, Age 65, Marble, North Carolina

Prayers for me were answered when bedridden with cancer.
Loretta, Age 64, Hickory, North Carolina

I was told I was cured of cancer.
Lynn, Age 67, North Carolina

I met my husband for the first time.
Lisa, Age 45, Durham, North Carolina

I lost a teenaged friend in a car accident.
Age 56, Kings Mountain, North Carolina

I had surgery for cancer.
Kinard, Age 79, Salisbury, North Carolina
In my darkest hour He took over without my asking.
Paula, Age 59, Charlotte, North Carolina

I hold the hand of a dying person.
Lori, Age 45, Salisbury, North Carolina

I was arrested for a DWI.
Jim, Age 57, Alamance, North Carolina

Whenever I pray and read His Word.
Shirley

I fall asleep and rest.
Vicki, Age 62, Kannapolis, North Carolina

A butterfly landed on my knee in a crowded stadium.
Wade, Age 41, Hickory, North Carolina

I struggle to prepare a sermon.
Bob, Age 63, Hickory, North Carolina

I am watching my daughter sleep peacefully.
Mark, Age 43, Apex, North Carolina

I was free of my cancer.
Debbie, Age 57, Southern Pines, North Carolina

My wife smiles each morning.
Robert, Age 74, Stantonsburg, North Carolina

Our daughter graduated from Lutheran Theological Southern Seminary.
Sylvia, Age 69, Hickory, North Carolina

Each of our children was born.
Roger, Age 65, Burlington, North Carolina

He gave me the gift of my loving husband, Steve.
Delana, Age 55, Gastonia, North Carolina

My daughter, Lydia, was born – a miracle baby!
Jenni, Age 37, Gastonia, North Carolina

I have peace in hurtful situations.
Bill, Age 42, Gastonia, North Carolina

I spend time with youth on mission trips.
Steve, Age 57, Gastonia, North Carolina

I hear just the "Word" I most need to hear.
Janice, Age 69, Havelock, North Carolina

My mother died.
Nancy, Age 53, New Bern, North Carolina

I saw a rainbow when my mother-in-law died.
Cindy, Age 46, Charlotte, North Carolina

I made it through seminary.
Susan, Age 52, China Grove, North Carolina

I watch my children sleeping peacefully.
Stayce, Age 34, Holly Springs, North Carolina

We began our life together as husband and wife.
John, Age 69, Granite Falls, North Carolina

My children were born.
David, Age 75, Hickory, North Carolina

I saw a rainbow after a violent storm.
Anne, Age 72, Hickory, North Carolina

Grace trumps rules and laws even in God's Word.
Dennis, Age 64, Hickory, North Carolina

I read my mother's favorite Psalm after her death.
Susan, Age 67, Granite Falls, North Carolina

I survived Girl Scout camp as the leader.
Cheryl, Age 65, Cherryville, North Carolina

My friend fell at age 93 and was not hurt.
Tim, Age 66, Cherryville, North Carolina

I walked the journey of Papa's death.
Bea, Age 61, Newton, North Carolina

I had a wonderful family.
Al, Age 73, Hickory, North Carolina

I see your beautiful face and smile each day.
Rosebud, Age 70, Raleigh, North Carolina

Each of my children was born.
Eric, Age 37, Taylorsville, North Carolina

I talk to Him on the way to work.
Jeff, Age 38, Arden, North Carolina

Jesus held me prior to cancer surgery.
David, Age 59, Asheville, North Carolina

My mother was taken to Heaven unexpectedly in an accident.
Marilyn, Age 47, Sanford, North Carolina

My husband was dying.
Pat, Age 65, Greensboro, North Carolina

My husband passed on to the life triumphant.
Ethel, Age 80, Hickory, North Carolina

My son died at age 18.
Don, Age 64, Salisbury, North Carolina

I held my newly-baptized son in my arms.
Joe, Age 58, Concord, North Carolina

My son returned home after a long separation.
Helen, Age 70, Pinehurst, North Carolina

I meet weekly with my Stephen Ministry Care Receiver.
Skip, Age 73, Hendersonville, North Carolina

Our family shared good memories of my deceased daughter.
Bob, Age 75, Hendersonville, North Carolina

I cared for my mother until her death.
Barbara, Age 53, Newton, North Carolina

My mother died of cancer and dad died of ALS.
Brenda, Age 60, Hickory, North Carolina

My mother died.
Bill, Age 62, Newton, North Carolina

We found out my dad had cancer.
Gretchen, Age 46, Mt. Holly, North Carolina

I find a convenient parking place at a crowded mall.
Mike, Age 57, Mt. Holly, North Carolina

I breathe in the life-giving love of God.
Sue, Age 63, Charlotte, North Carolina

I served 60 years as an ordained minister.
Charles, Age 83

I spend time with my children, grandchildren and great-grandchildren.
Norma, Age 72, Hickory, North Carolina

The IRS did not take my home for back taxes.
Marty, Age 57, Dallas, North Carolina

I was accepted into Vet Med School.
Katrina, Age 49, Greensboro, North Carolina

My 15-year-old daughter survived an LSD trip.
Richard, Age 63

I received a new heart valve.
John, Age 48, Salisbury, North Carolina

I care for my elderly father whose health is failing.
Karen, Age 53, Boone, North Carolina

I marvel at how our gracious Lord answers prayers.
Rita, Age 55, Salisbury, North Carolina

He comforted me when my dad died.
Jeanette, Age 53, Burlington, North Carolina

I am alone with the sounds of nature.
Bob, Age 74, Claremont, North Carolina

I wake to another day to share the Gospel.
Camille, Age 54, Conover, North Carolina

Our children were born.
Phil, Age 40, Salisbury, North Carolina

My mom was diagnosed with breast cancer.
Jennifer, Age 34, Kannapolis, North Carolina

I heard the call to teaching ministry.
Sharon, Age 38, Taylorsville, North Carolina

I was badly burned when I was 3 years old.
Carrie, Age 55, Salisbury, North Carolina

God called me to seminary at age 41.
Angela, Age 46, Charlotte, North Carolina

I crocheted baptismal blankets for my granddaughter and grandson.
Ron, Age 59, Conover, North Carolina

I "lost my life" in an accident 54 years ago.
Ann, Age 71, Conover, North Carolina

I walked into Susan's hospital room and she exclaimed, "They just took my baby – she stopped breathing."
Greg, Age 50, Hendersonville, North Carolina

My wife died.
Bill, Age 68, Hickory, North Carolina

I give thanks for being a cancer survivor.
Ann, Age 70, Lincolnton, North Carolina

I was feeling sorry for myself.
Robert, Age 56, Lincolnton, North Carolina

I helped with hurricane relief in Mississippi.
Darrell, Age 62, Salisbury, North Carolina

I play in the ocean.
Stacie, Age 50, Charlotte, North Carolina

I sense calm in a hard situation.
David, Age 50, CHL, North Carolina

A child asked to say the prayer at a meeting.
Derek, Age 43, Lexington, North Carolina

My grandchild was born.
Cathy, Age 68, Kannapolis, North Carolina

I survived life-threatening cancer surgery.
John, Age 76, Kannapolis, North Carolina

I gathered with sisters and brothers to receive communion.
Gary, Age 46, Lincolnton, North Carolina

My daughter said her first prayer.
Andrew, Age 31, Taylorsville, North Carolina

I married a pastor even though I said I wouldn't.
Dot, Age 69, New London, North Carolina

I entered every structure fire as a firefighter.
Melvin, Age 48, Mooresville, North Carolina

I hear my children sing praise and worship songs.
Penny, Age 38, Salisbury, North Carolina

I gave thanks for the birth of my child.
Don, Age 55, Salisbury, North Carolina

I went over the pit wall for the first time.
Chris, Age 44, Gold Hill, North Carolina

A young man reassured me after an auto accident.
Sue, Age 65, High Point, North Carolina

My husband suddenly took his own life.
Ann, Age 66, Conover, North Carolina

My 14-year-old son took his own life.
Tom, Age 64, Hickory, North Carolina

Cancer was overcome.
Sarah, Age 70, Salisbury, North Carolina

I had my children, and I learned I had cancer.
Geraldine, Age 71, Salisbury, North Carolina

My daughter was born not breathing and I baptized her.
Paul, Age 67, Hickory, North Carolina

I met my wonderful wife.
Daniel, Age 30, Gibsonville, North Carolina

I'm out in God's creation and in our vegetable garden.
Larry, Age 67, Lexington, North Carolina

I sit on a mountain and watch the sun set.
Judy, Age 66, Lexington, North Carolina

I found out I was pregnant!
Virginia, Age 27, Gibsonville, North Carolina

God gave me the strength to work towards my goals.
Sarah, Age 24, Thomasville, North Carolina

I met my first Care Receiver as a Stephen Minister.
Gordon, Age 60, Raleigh, North Carolina

I care for someone struggling with a health issue.
John, Age 65, Concord, North Carolina

My two grandchildren were born.
John, Age 65, Concord, North Carolina

I landed in Dover, Delaware from Vietnam.
Nathan, Age 65, Asheboro, North Carolina

I first stood at the brink of Yellowstone Lower Falls.
Ben, Age 64, Salisbury, North Carolina

He let me live to see Nick believe.
Marie, Age 60, Monroe, North Carolina

Our relationship was transformed into a beautiful marriage.
Donna, Age 61, Cary, North Carolina

I had my first child.
Barbara, Age 55, Cary, North Carolina

My daughter was uninjured after being hit by two trucks.
Pat, Age 69, Hudson, North Carolina

I stand at the edge of the ocean and listen.
Pat, Age 66, Salisbury, North Carolina

"Jesus help me" gave me peace after an accident.
Peggy, Age 61, Salisbury, North Carolina

I felt his presence during the trials of motherhood.
Carolyn, Age 67, Dallas, North Carolina

I experienced peace during the stillborn birth of my grandson.
Becky, Age 56, Washington, North Carolina

I live my bipolar life with prayer, medication and Him!
Jeanette, Age 61, Lexington, North Carolina

I was in the right place to save my great-niece.
Lori, Age 50, Wingate, North Carolina

My son's birth when I was 16 saved my life.
Savannah, Age 23, Marshville, North Carolina

He reminded me of His presence during turmoil.
Rhoda, Age 72, Etowah, North Carolina

I first had cancer and my church provided.
Judy, Age 63, Durham, North Carolina

I pray for God to keep me awake while driving.
Marvene, Age 61, Kannapolis, North Carolina

I turned and started my way back home to Him.
Donna, Age 63, Gibsonville, North Carolina

He reassured me after I found out I had cancer.
Donna, Age 42, Mt. Pleasant

A tree fell inches from my vehicle. God protected me!
Michelle

Every time I look at someone smiling over another's joy.
Shelby

I look up and see the sun shining behind the clouds.
Emily

I realized that people love me for who I am, not who I was pretending to be.
A.C.

Mugged on a train, had food poisoning, traveled home from Europe.
Laura

I was deployed to Iraq.
Tara

I first saw the man who is soon to be my husband.
Brittany

In New Orleans thousands of kids sang worship songs outside spontaneously. *Thomas*

I cried endlessly that day before my nursing boards.
Katy

Loved ones were in the hospital
Hunter

Lying on the beach and I saw nothing but miles of water.
Amanda

My family ate together, even when mad at each other.
Banks

A worship meeting strengthened and comforted me by God's peace. *Joseph*

On a beautiful vast mountaintop, I was humbled but at peace.
Wesley

My husband and I felt called to start a new congregation in Sioux Falls. *Suzanne*

I decided to move home from college for a "fresh start"
Carrie

I decided where to go to college.
Emily

When I was pressured by my peers.
Nathan, Age 15, Hickory, North Carolina

When my dog Spicey became an important part of my life.
Margaret, Age 88, Hickory, North Carolina

Courting my future wife and asking God's guidance and blessing.
Paul, Age 57, Hickory, North Carolina

When I applied to seminary.
Joel, Age 30, St. Paul, Minnesota

I see despair transformed into new life.
Sarah, Age 26, St. Paul, Minnesota

JOURNAL YOUR NEW GRAND MEMORY WAVES: